P9-BTO-250

HIGH-TECH
WEAPONS

o o o o

WRITTEN BY

JOHN ALLEN

BLACKBIRCH PRESS

An imprint of Thomson Gale, a part of The Thomson Corporation

WITHDRAWAL

THOMSON
GALE

Property of
FAUQUIER COUNTY PUBLIC LIBRARY
11 Winchester Street
Warrenton, VA 20186

Detroit • New York • San Francisco • San Diego • New Haven, Conn. • Waterville, Maine • London • Munich

THOMSON

✳ ™

GALE

© 2005 Thomson Gale, a part of the Thomson Corporation.

Thomson and Star Logo are trademarks and Gale and Blackbirch Press are registered trademarks used herein under license.

For more information, contact
Blackbirch Press
27500 Drake Rd.
Farmington Hills, MI 48331-3535
Or you can visit our Internet site at http://www.gale.com

ALL RIGHTS RESERVED
No part of this work covered by the copyright hereon may be reproduced or used in any form or by any means—graphic, electronic, or mechanical, including photocopying, recording, taping, Web distribution, or information storage retrieval systems—without the written permission of the publisher.

Every effort has been made to trace the owners of copyrighted material.

Photo credits: Cover: Aero Graphics, Inc/CORBIS, AP/Wide World Photos, 27, 33, 36,Center for Disease Control and Prevention, 30, © Bettmann/CORBIS, 16, 21, © Horace Bristol/CORBIS, 6, © Chris Carroll/COR-BIS, 42, © Ed Kashi/CORBIS, 5, © Hulton-Deutsch Collection/CORBIS, 10, 12, © Lester Lefkowitz/CORBIS, 32, © Michael Macor/San Francisco Chronicle/CORBIS, 27 (inset), © Ross Pictures/CORBIS, 17, © Peter Russell/The Military Picture Library/CORBIS, 22, © Jim Sugar/CORBIS, 14, © CORBIS, 7, 11, 38, Corel, 9 (both), Department of Defense, 13, 26, © Mark Abraham/EPA/Landov, 35, © Michael Ammons/UPI/Landov, 31, © Reuters/Landov, 23, © Radu Sighetti/Reuters/Landov, 19, Courtesy of NASA, 28, National Archives, 8, 15, Photos.com, 40, © Andrzej Dodzinski/Photo Researchers.com, 18

LIBRARY OF CONGRESS CATALOGING-IN-PUBLICATION DATA

Allen, John, 1957–
  High-tech weapons / by John Allen.
    p. cm. — (Science on the edge)
  Includes bibliographical references and index.
  ISBN 1-4103-0531-7 (hardcover : alk. paper)
  1. Military weapons—History. I. Title. II. Series.

U800.A427 2005
355.8'09—dc22   2004020648

Printed in the United States
10 9 8 7 6 5 4 3 2 1

FROM CATAPULTS TO CRUISE MISSILES

The history of the human race is filled with wars and conquests. Some wars are won with clever strategy or by good fortune. Most often, however, the winning side has superior technology—that is, more effective weapons.

For example, in the Battle of Agincourt (1415), Henry V's English army defeated the much more numerous French mainly because of a tactical weapon, the longbow. Five thousand English archers massed on two flanks fired volleys of arrows that darkened the skies. The longbow attacks sowed confusion and allowed the English to carry the day.

Throughout history, each new weapon or mode of defense has led to some new weapon to counter it. Just as the ancient Greeks used catapults to attack fortresses, modern armies use antiaircraft guns to fire on bombers and warplanes. Today, scientists are working on systems to counter missile attacks with lasers or other missiles.

An Afghan soldier mans an antiaircraft machine gun. Advanced weapons have helped win wars throughout history.

Modern-day soldiers use computers to guide weapons to faraway targets.

Going as far back as 1864, when General William T. Sherman's Union army laid waste to Southern cities, the modern age has seen the advent of so-called total war, in which neither civilians nor cities are spared. In 1940, Adolf Hitler's German bombers turned London into a firestorm. In 1945, the United States dropped the atom bomb on the Japanese cities of Hiroshima and Nagasaki. Since then, there have been efforts to develop weapons that limit the number of human casualties and minimize the destruction. Computers, lasers, and satellites allow new weapons to strike faraway targets with remarkable precision. A new class of nonlethal weapons aims to incapacitate opponents without killing or seriously injuring them.

Technologically advanced weapons—high-tech weapons— continue to change the way that wars are fought. Some experts hope these advances will actually reduce the number of wars in the future. What is certain, however, is that future victories on the battlefield will begin in the laboratory.

CHAPTER 1

TECHNOLOGY MEETS MODERN WARFARE

World War I saw the use of modern weapons in a crude form. In many ways, however, World War II was the first high-tech war. After the long, bloody sieges of World War I, weapons makers changed their strategy. They hoped that faster, more powerful weapons might bring the next war to a conclusion more quickly. To that end, they designed machines more deadly than any seen before. Most of the new weapons were designed for offense, but breakthroughs in defense and communications were also made.

Nations used their industrial know-how to create arsenals of new weapons, including aircraft, battleships, submarines, tanks, artillery guns, hand grenades, and, finally, nuclear weapons. These weapons were designed to cause the greatest amount of destruction possible. As a result, the number of civilian deaths during World War II was unprecedented. For example, one of America's most effective weapons in the war was the bomber. This plane dropped massive numbers of bombs

Weapons makers produced many new weapons in World War II, including advanced aircraft.

The Germans in World War II used new technologies in the Panzer tank (pictured) to help fight their "lightning war."

over a targeted area—a strategy that became known as carpet bombing. Carpet bombing was not very accurate, and large numbers of casualties could not be avoided. In the 1945 Allied bombing of Dresden, Germany, nearly 25,000 homes were destroyed, and casualty estimates were in the tens of thousands.

WEAPONS OF WORLD WAR II

On the other side, Nazi Germany used many of the new technologies in a tactic called blitzkrieg, or "lightning war." The idea was to attack the enemy so rapidly and with so much force that it could not defend itself. Speedy new fighter and bomber planes began the attack against enemy positions. Dive-bombers would dive directly at a target to drop bombs more accurately. Fighter planes would strafe enemy troops with machine guns.

Next came a combined force of tanks and armored personnel carriers. The German Panzer IV tank weighed 17 tons and was

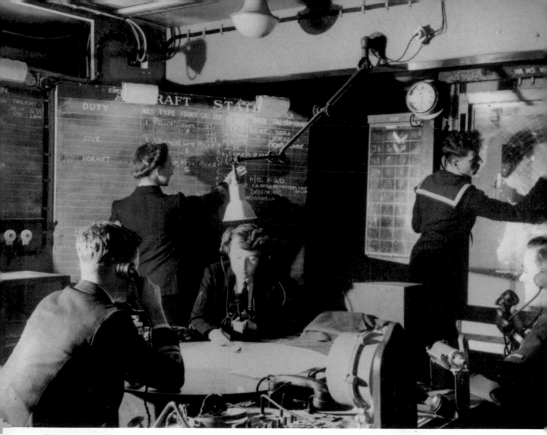

British soldiers use radar to track the movement of German aircraft.

equipped with a 75mm turret gun and two machine guns. Despite its weight, it could travel 18 miles (29km) per hour over almost any terrain. (Panzers and other tanks were even employed in the deserts of northern Africa.)

The movements of these armored vehicles were coordinated by another new invention—portable two-way radios. As German forces drove deep into enemy territory at great speed, individual commanders used radios to keep up with and adapt to changing conditions on the battlefield. Sometimes paratroopers, or troops with parachutes, would be dropped behind enemy lines. Using blitzkrieg attacks, smaller forces could render much larger armies helpless in a matter of days.

Germany was not the only country to make use of new advances in weaponry. German air attacks in England were countered by another recently developed technology. To detect enemy aircraft, the

British used radar, or radio detection and ranging. Radar devices sent out radio waves that bounced off airplanes and revealed their positions. By the end of the war, British radar had increased in range from 8 miles (12.8km) to 40 miles (64.3km).

The British also pioneered cryptography, or the use of codes for secret messages. Electronic machines stationed at military headquarters would send messages in a complex code that could be decoded only by a similar machine. Machines were also developed to decode enemy communications. A British code machine called Colossus, a forerunner of the computer, helped break the main German code, Ultra. The messages that were intercepted and decoded gave the Allies important tips about enemy troop movements and strategies.

Japan, too, introduced new weapons during the war. One of the most effective was the Type 0 Carrier Fighter, or Zero. The Zero was the best fighter plane of its era, with the ability to fly long distances and outmaneuver enemy planes. For example, the Zero had a range of 1,200 miles (1,931km) without refueling, compared to the 850-mile (1,367km) range of its chief American adversary, the P-40 Warhawk. The Zero's relatively small size enabled it to make tight turns and steep climbs that no other fighter plane of the time could match. Scores of Zero fighters

The American P-40 Warhawk (top) was no match for the long-range Japanese Zero (bottom).

The wooden LCVP allowed the Allies to establish beachheads in the D-Day invasion.

were deployed from the decks of aircraft carriers. The planes could take off and land on these massive air bases in the ocean, giving them even greater range for attack. Japanese pilots sometimes made kamikaze attacks, crashing their planes into enemy carriers in a fiery suicide mission.

While the Japanese improved weapons in the air, the United States made advances on land. To move troops and equipment rapidly onto coastlines, American inventors built wooden boats called LCVPs (which stood for Landing Craft, Vehicle, Personnel). A single LCVP could land a platoon of 36 soldiers with full equipment or a jeep and 12 soldiers, extract itself from the sand with the help of half-tracks (wide rubber tracks on a drive system of wheels), and then return to a carrier for more men and equipment. LCVPs enabled Allied troops to establish beachheads at the D-Day invasion of Normandy. Otherwise, the Allies would have been forced to capture a port city to obtain wharves and docks for unloading troops.

ROCKETS AND BOMBS

In addition to the new weapons that were introduced, World War II also saw an increase in the killing power of long-range explosives. In 1942, Nazi Germany began work on two secret weapons that it hoped to use as terror weapons to demoralize Allied civilians. Both were precursors to today's guided missiles. The first to be deployed was the V-1 flying bomb, a pilotless single-wing aircraft that carried a 1-ton warhead, or bomb. Despite its advanced design, the V-1 could not fly above the range of antiaircraft guns. Almost half of the flying Bombs launched against southern England were shot down.

Germany designed the V-1 flying bomb as a terror weapon to demoralize Allied civilians.

The flawed guidance system of the V-2 rocket kept it from becoming a significant Nazi weapon.

An improved version, the V-2 rocket, was developed next. The 45-foot-long (13.7m) V-2 could fly at supersonic speeds, faster than any other object of its time, and reach an altitude of 50 miles (80.4 km), making it impossible to stop once launched. Plunging from the upper atmosphere with a screaming roar, this weapon was a terrifying reminder of Germany's technological advances. However, the V-2's guidance system proved inadequate. From 200 miles (321 km) away, it could reliably hit only a target the size of a city. Of the 5,000 V-2 rockets fired at England, about 80 percent never reached their targets. Introduced only months before the war's end, the V-2 never became a significant weapon for the Nazis.

Meanwhile, the United States was developing its own secret weapon. This effort, dubbed the Manhattan Project, sought to harness the explosive power of the atom. The United States recruited scientists from around the world to work on the project. The physicist Albert Einstein had suggested forming such a research team to President Franklin D. Roosevelt before the war.

Scientists worked feverishly, first to isolate nuclear material from uranium and plutonium, then to develop a workable weapon using this material. The first atomic bomb was tested at Los Alamos, New Mexico, on July 6, 1945. A month later, two nuclear bombs were exploded over the Japanese cities of Hiroshima and Nagasaki. More than one hundred thousand people were killed instantly, and thousands more died later from various effects of the blast. American leaders contended that the bombs ended the war in Japan more quickly and prevented even larger numbers of casualties on both sides. Nevertheless, the decision to use atomic weapons had many critics. Some thought technology was out of control and feared what new weapons might be created next.

The atomic bomb explodes over Hiroshima. The United States brought scientists from around the world to work on the weapon.

CHAPTER 2

STRATEGIC WEAPONS OF TODAY

In the years following World War II, the Cold War between the United States and the Soviet Union led both sides to build nuclear arsenals. Nevertheless, since 1945, atomic weapons have not been used. Both sides were restrained by a policy called MAD, or mutually assured destruction. Since both had missiles that could reach enemy cities in minutes, neither side could afford to launch the first strike. Smaller regional conflicts did occur, however, and technology continued to play an important part in these wars.

The U.S. Air Force developed the Sabre fighter jet to counter the North Koreans' MiG. The plane featured improved speed and maneuverability over previous jets.

An American soldier aims a Super Bazooka. The weapon used an electrical current to launch a rocket.

JETS, ROCKET LAUNCHERS, AND NAPALM

One such conflict was the Korean War, which began in 1950 and was fought between Communist North Korea and United Nations forces. After World War II, many U.S. military leaders thought that nuclear weapons would make ground warfare obsolete. As a result, production of new battlefield weapons lagged until late in the Korean conflict, and the war was fought mostly with surplus weapons from World War II. There were, however, innovations in aircraft. The U.S. Air Force introduced the Sabre fighter jet to counter the North Koreans' MiG. With their swept-back wing design and powerful engines, both planes had greater maneuverability and could fly higher and faster than previous aircraft. U.S. bombing missions were aided by C-47 "Lightning Bugs," which dropped parachute flares that illuminated nighttime targets with five minutes of brilliant light.

The Korean War ended in 1953. In the next major conflict, the Vietnam War, both sides used rocket launchers to destroy tanks and

A Chinook helicopter brings in supplies. Americans used Chinooks to attack enemy soldiers hidden in forests during the Vietnam War.

helicopters. These weapons were improved versions of the bazooka, a World War II–era firearm that shot grenades. The U.S. version of the rocket launcher, called the Super Bazooka, required a two-man team and had a range of more than 3,900 feet (1,200m). A rocket was loaded into a long tube and two wires were attached to electrical batteries. When the trigger was pulled, an electrical current set off the rocket motor to propel the rocket forward. A danger of this weapon was the deadly back-blast that exploded from the rear of the launcher tube.

Heavy foliage in Vietnam provided ideal cover for the guerrilla fighters of the Vietcong. New weapons to flush them out into the open included the Chinook helicopter, which could hover just above the tree line and attack with machine guns. U.S. planes also sprayed chemicals called defoliants to kill the vegetation. One defoliant, called Agent Orange, was later found to have serious effects on the health of those exposed to it.

Another controversial weapon was called napalm. As far back as World War I, armies had tried to use gasoline in flamethrowers. However, it burned itself out too quickly to be effective. In 1942, the U.S. Army invented napalm, which was a jellied mixture of aluminum soap powder and gasoline. Napalm bombs, or incendiary bombs, would explode into fire on impact. Napalm bombs were used against Dresden and cities in Japan. In Vietnam, a new form of napalm was used to reduce acres of trees to smoke and ash as well as to terrorize enemy cities and villages.

Canisters of napalm await use. The U.S. military used napalm against enemy targets during the Vietnam War.

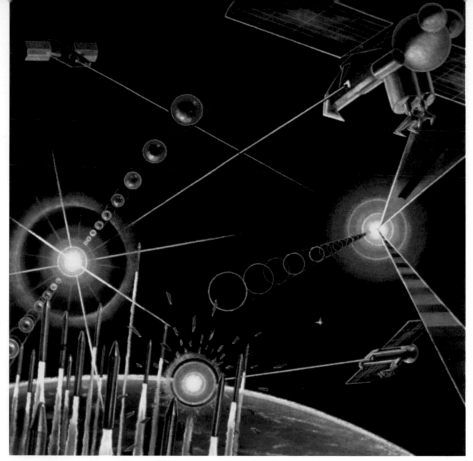

An artist's drawing shows SDI weapons in action. President Reagan's 1983 plan for space-based weapons never became a reality.

The Vietnam War ended in 1979, but the Cold War continued. In a bid to win this war once and for all, the United States undertook a massive arms buildup in the 1980s. The buildup included conventional weapons and improved missiles, but also saw the development of new space-age technologies. In 1983, President Ronald Reagan announced his Strategic Defense Initiative (SDI) to develop space-based weapons that could shoot down enemy missiles. This would be accomplished, in theory, by satellites equipped with lasers or other kinds of weapons. The program became known as "Star Wars," after the science-fiction movie. While SDI was never built (and, according to critics, could not have been built), some of the ideas it included are used in high-tech weapons of today.

GLOBAL POSITIONING SYSTEM (GPS)

The first step in using space technology for military purposes was the invention of the satellite, an unmanned spacecraft that could be launched into Earth orbit. The first satellite, a basketball-sized device called *Sputnik I*, was launched by the Soviet Union in 1957. Soon the United States began launching its own satellites. Scientists quickly learned that they could track the orbit of a satellite with radio waves. This discovery, in turn, led to the creation of a sophisticated system for tracking objects on Earth: the Global Positioning System (GPS).

The Soviet Union launched the first satellite, *Sputnik I* (pictured), into orbit in 1957.

THE PATRIOT MISSILE

One of the high-tech success stories of the Persian Gulf War was the Patriot missile system. It showed the capability

A Patriot missile lifts off from its launcher.

to do something that President Ronald Reagan had hoped for with the Strategic Defense Initiative: shoot down a missile with another missile.

As expected, Iraq attacked coalition forces and the nation of Israel with Scud missiles. The Patriot system had great success in intercepting the Scuds and destroying them on impact, thus potentially saving hundreds of lives.

A Patriot missile battery, or weapons group, has up to sixteen launchers, each roughly the size of a tractor-trailer. There are two kinds of Patriot missiles. The PAC-2 is designed to explode into fragments near the target to knock it off course. The PAC-3 actually hits the incoming target and destroys it completely—"hitting a bullet with a bullet," as experts say.

The Patriot system works by scanning the area for incoming missiles with powerful radar. When it finds a target, it communicates with the Patriot command center. There, technicians track the status of all the targets that the system has found. Technicians can choose to let the Patriot system operate automatically or can select or delete targets themselves.

When a target is identified as an enemy rocket, the command center downloads guidance data to a Patriot missile and launches it. With the PAC-2, the command center continues to track the incoming rocket, and also tracks the Patriot, giving it constant updates on its heading and speed. The technicians steer the outbound Patriot until it is close enough to the target to detonate.

The PAC-3 is able to guide itself with its own radar and computer. Once fired, it adjusts its own course toward the target. At maximum speed, it approaches the enemy rocket at Mach 10, which is 2.1 miles (3.4km) per second. There is little margin for error, whether by the human operator or from a computer glitch—an error of one-hundreth of a second throws the Patriot off target by more than 100 feet (30.5m).

The Patriot system has also had high-profile failures. Early in the second Iraq War, a Patriot missile misidentified a British jet and destroyed it. This incident led to questions about whether weapons like the Patriot that work automatically are ready for battlefield use.

The GPS uses a constellation of twenty four satellites in space as reference points for locations on Earth. A GPS device receives radio signals from three satellites. It instantly measures the precise distance from the three satellites to the receiver's location on or above the planet's surface. Using a mathematical method called triangulation, this data is used to fix the exact location of that point—its latitude, longitude, and altitude. The GPS can track the position of anything on Earth at any time and in any weather—and it is accurate to within a few meters. It is even used in cars and boats to help drivers and sailors who are lost.

During the Persian Gulf War, GPS receivers like this one helped soldiers navigate through sandstorms and darkness.

In the 1990s, the GPS became an essential military tool. During the Persian Gulf War, which took place in Iraq and Kuwait in 1991, coalition forces employed the system to navigate in blinding sandstorms and in darkness. Aircraft, ships, and foot soldiers all depended on the GPS to coordinate their movements. By war's end, more than 9,000 GPS receivers—many no larger than a cell phone—were in use in the conflict.

SMART WEAPONS

Along with satellites, lasers also play a vital role in high-tech warfare. A laser is a device that generates a concentrated, directional beam of light. Lasers can be used to guide a weapon to its target with uncanny accuracy. Aided by computer microchips, laser-guided bombs are often called smart weapons. Because they are so accurate, they often require less explosive power than conventional bombs dropped from the air to destroy a target. This in turn creates less collateral damage, or harm to surrounding structures and civilians.

U.S. forces used laser-guided bombs in Vietnam, and the British employed a more sophisticated version in the 1982 Falklands War. The first widespread use, however, came in the Persian Gulf War. Eyewitnesses described bombs that would glide in precise paths around buildings and other obstacles, even turning corners to reach

A Tomahawk cruise missile launches from a guided missile cruiser. The Tomahawk is one of America's most sophisticated high-tech weapons.

their targets. U.S. commanders displayed videos showing remarkably accurate "hits" due to guided weapons. However, some of this success was overstated. One danger of smart weapons is that if a signal is jammed or a mechanical part does not work, a bomb can travel far off target, causing unintentional damage.

One kind of smart weapon depends on targets being painted, or illuminated, by a laser. The target can be painted by soldiers on the ground or by aircraft. The painted target designator then leads the weapon to its goal with a coded pulse of energy that only the weapon's system can read. In poor weather, however, or in situations where no target designator can be provided, the weapon is rarely used. Rain, fog, smoke, dust, and debris can all interfere with the effectiveness of laser-guided bombs.

Another kind of smart weapon relies on the GPS system for guidance. The Joint Direct Attack Munition (JDAM) is a guidance kit added to the tail of an old-style bomb. The JDAM allows the bomb to be directed to a precise target by use of GPS data. Bad weather and other harsh conditions have no effect on the JDAM.

The GPS also guides Tomahawk cruise missiles. The Tomahawk flies very low and can even be reprogrammed midflight. It can hover above a target and, using an onboard camera, send back information about previous damage to a target before proceeding with its own strike. First used in the Persian Gulf War with great success, the Tomahawk has become the premier high-tech weapon in the U.S. arsenal. In the Iraq War of 2003, U.S. submarines and ships launched Tomahawk missiles against military targets in Baghdad and other cities.

CHAPTER 3

HIGH-TECH WEAPONS OF TOMORROW

Many weapons of the future will be controlled remotely or preprogrammed by computer. This will allow an army to inflict damage on an enemy without endangering its own soldiers. Some new weapons, such as battlefield lasers, might resemble something in a science-fiction movie. Other new weapons are based on technologies never dreamed of before.

DRONES AND ROBOTS FOR RECONNAISSANCE

Many new weapon technologies are designed not to kill but to acquire information. Information about the enemy is always key to winning a battle. The process of gathering this information is called reconnaissance. In ancient times, scouts on foot spied on enemy camps. More recently, spy planes and satellites have been used to track troop movements. In the future, these missions will be done by a variety of unmanned vehicles and robot drones.

The U.S. Air Force already uses a pilotless long-range aircraft to spy on the enemy. Called the Predator, this plane carries three video cameras that transmit images. One of these cameras is an infrared model that operates in very low light. The Predator also is equipped with a radar camera for peering through clouds, smoke, or haze. Soon, troops on the ground will be able to access video from the Predator on laptop computers. This will instantly give them pictures of the developing battlefield. In turn commanders will be able to direct the Predator to fire on ground targets.

The Predator, however, may one day seem bulky and clumsy compared to the new Micro Air Vehicles, or MAVs. An MAV is no

The U.S. Air Force uses the pilotless, long-range Predator to spy on enemy positions.

larger than a model airplane, yet it is well equipped. Microtechnology, or the science of making things very small, allows each MAV to be loaded with useful tools. One MAV features a camera, communications gear, a chemical sensor for detecting poison gas, and even tiny weapons. A group of these minidrones, like a flock of birds, could peek over hilltops at enemy formations or spy on terrorist camps from close by. They would be ideal for exploring in areas that might be contaminated with gas or some other deadly material. They could even search for survivors in a collapsed building.

An MAV is designed to fly two hours at 90 miles (144.8km)per hour. It is powered by miniature fuel cell batteries and guided by a lightweight satellite system. It can be launched by hand, shot from a weapon, or dropped from another aircraft.

A ground version of the MAV is the Packbot, which was used in the Iraq War. The Packbot is a remote-controlled robot that looks like a toy tank on half-tracks. Equipped with a video camera and sensors, it can climb stairs and maneuver around obstacles. Packbot operators use the robot to search for mines and booby traps in areas where the enemy has been. One version of the Packbot, called Dragon Eyes, weighs just over 5 pounds (2.26kg) and fits inside a backpack.

A MAV (below) can be launched by hand to perform a variety of tasks. The Packbot (inset), a ground version of the MAV, is used to search for mines and booby traps.

ANTISATELLITE WEAPONS

High-tech warfare depends on electronic communications. With this in mind, military planners are looking at ways to win battles by knocking out these capabilities at the start.

For example, the People's Republic of China is working on several weapons designed to attack military communications and weapons guidance systems. The overall effort is called "counterspace" by military experts. This refers to the notion that the most important battles of the future may be fought in outer space, as antagonists try to destroy each other's space technology.

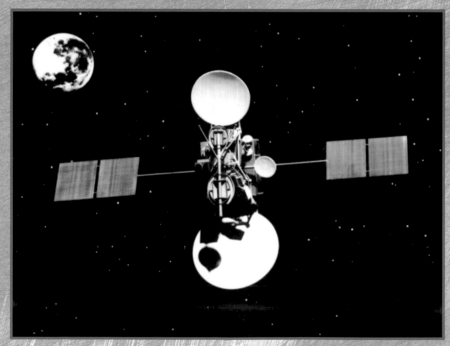

Antisatellite weapons target satellites
like this to keep them from operating.

ASATs, or antisatellite weapons, are any system designed to destroy a satellite or keep it from operating. Some ASATs seek to damage enemy satellites with a powerful laser or with nuclear missiles. Without satellites, weapons and other devices that operate on the Global Positioning System would be useless. Thus blinded, a modern army would have to rely on old-fashioned weapons that are much less effective. It would also lose its advantage in planning and coordination.

There might be simpler ways to disable a satellite without using weapons in space. The U.S. space shuttle has been used to retrieve the orbiting Hubble telescope for repairs. Experts point out that it could just as easily pluck an enemy satellite from its orbit. Also, a competing electronic signal could be used to jam a satellite's communications. A satellite might be bombarded with incorrect data, a tactic called "spoofing." Finally, forces could attack the ground station that controls a satellite, rendering the system just as useless as if the satellite were destroyed.

To counter a strike in space, China and other nations are working on microsatellites and nanosatellites. These very small satellites, some weighing as little as 50 pounds (22.6kg), could be used to provide backups if one system is damaged or knocked out. They might also serve as a flock of decoys to confuse an attacker. Certainly, the competition in satellites and space technology is only beginning.

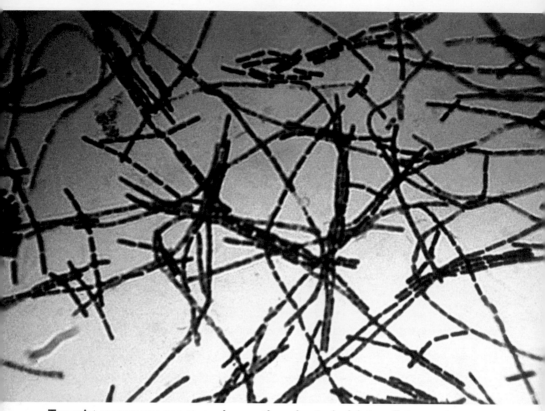

Terrorist groups use agents such as anthrax bacteria (pictured) to create biological weapons.

BOMBS OF THE FUTURE

One of the functions of Packbots and drones is to locate chemical and biological weapons that might be stockpiled by terrorist groups or rogue governments. Chemical weapons are designed to introduce toxic chemicals or gases into enemy military or civilian populations. Biological weapons attack the enemy with deadly bacteria, such as anthrax, or viruses, such as Ebola. Outlawed by international treaty, these weapons have the potential to cause great harm to civilians. Planners are looking at ways to destroy these weapons before they can be used.

One possible solution is the thermo-corrosive bomb. This bomb is actually a filling added to other 2,000-pound (907kg) "bunker-busting" explosives. The filling burns at 1,000°F

(537.7°C) for several minutes, long enough to consume the contents of an underground bunker in which biological or chemical weapons might be stored. Despite the intense heat, the thermo-corrosive bomb keeps the overall pressure of the bunker low, preventing dangerous chemicals from shooting out before they are burned away.

Another new weapon is the microwave bomb, or E-bomb. (The E stands for electromagnetic.) It produces a burst of powerful microwaves, the same energy used to cook food in a microwave oven. This burst can disable electronic devices, wreck computer memories, and even disable car ignitions over a wide area. Such a weapon could knock out enemy radar and communications without an explosion. An E-bomb could be delivered by a robot drone or by

An American warplane releases a "bunker-busting" bomb. This bomb was designed to destroy the contents of underground bunkers.

The carbon filaments released by an exploding blackout bomb could disable this electrical plant in an instant.

a guided missile. Its effectiveness would be determined by the intensity of the waves produced and the proximity of the burst to its target. People in the area during an E-bomb attack would feel nothing.

Related to the E-bomb is a high-powered microwave cannon that shoots a microwave beam much like a laser beam. The beam can be focused on a particular target from miles away, such as a command post or computer center, to disrupt or disable radar and electronic devices. The batteries needed to power such a weapon are massive. However, experts hope to reduce the size of the power source and make the weapon portable in the future.

A third futuristic bomb is the blackout bomb. It releases a mass of carbon filaments like spider webs. These webs are made of a superconductive material that can disrupt power lines and power grids. Exploded over an electrical plant, a blackout bomb could disable its output in an instant.

BATTLEFIELD LASERS

Besides new bombs, high-tech inventors are also working on laser weapons that can defuse enemy rockets. The Tactical High Energy Laser (THEL) is a joint project of the United States and Israeli governments. Plagued by rocket attacks from rebel groups in its region, Israel hopes the weapon will succeed in protecting soldiers and civilians. Some claim that THEL could become the ultimate defensive weapon of the 21st century.

The new weapon operates on the same principle as the lasers in CD drives and DVD players. Light from a strong flashbulb directs a stream of photons into nine glass discs. Inside the discs, the light becomes concentrated into a beam of colorless light. The beam

The Tactical High Energy Laser (below) can heat steel from two hundred yards away. Scientists hope to develop it into a battlefield weapon.

emerges from the focusing crystal with the power to heat steel from 200 yards (182:8m) away. An electronic control system keeps the ray on target, while a computerized database tells it where to attack each enemy weapon—such as a guidance system or power source—for maximum effect.

Early tests have been successful using ten kilowatts of power at short range. However, more than one hundred kilowatts are needed to reach the goal of superheating and exploding enemy rockets at a distance of 5 miles (8km). At that power level, the weapon overheats and the system shuts down. Scientists are working on ways to rapidly cool the laser between firings to make it usable on the battlefield. While the current weapon resembles a massive searchlight and is mounted on a large platform or command post, engineers also hope to test a mobile version small enough to fit on a Humvee. Laser weapons might someday become as common as radar and antiaircraft guns for defense against attacks from the air.

CHAPTER 4

NONLETHAL WEAPONS OF TOMORROW

Today, research on new weapons is focused more than ever on nonlethal weapons. These are weapons designed not to kill but to incapacitate a person, rendering him or her unable to fight back. In modern warfare, soldiers often must fight in crowded areas where many innocent civilians live and work. The military and the police sometimes confront angry mobs. Nonlethal weapons allow them to use force without causing deaths or serious injuries.

The idea of nonlethal weapons is not new. Tear gas has long been used to break up riots or flush out suspects. Shot out of a rifle like launcher in projectiles that explode into thick clouds,

A police officer fires tear gas from a launcher. Tear gas is one of several weapons used to control crowds without causing serious injury or death.

tear gas causes a person's eyes to sting and water uncontrollably and makes it difficult to breathe. These effects are temporary, and the gas ceases to be a threat when it disperses. Pepper spray works in a similar way. It is made from the same chemicals found in jalapeño peppers, chemicals that can burn the inside of a person's mouth. Police have even used high-pressure water cannons to subdue adversaries without harming them. Scientists and engineers are working on even more effective nonlethal weapons for the future. Many of these are designed to assault one of the five senses. Electric shocks, deafening sounds, and foul smells might someday replace bullets and bombs in many dangerous situations.

A police officer aims a stun gun, an electric-shock weapon.

SWEEPING STUN GUNS

One challenge that law-enforcement officers frequently face is controlling unruly or dangerous crowds. In these situations, electric-shock weapons might be the answer. Electric-shock weapons are cannons that spray lightning bolts instead of water. They can stop crowds of people by sweeping them with a powerful beam of electricity. This technology is based on the success of the Taser, a handheld stun gun used by thousands of police departments in the United States. The Taser hits its victim with twin darts connected by a tiny wire that conducts electric current. The electric shock causes loss of balance and muscle control for five to ten minutes. However, the Taser works only at short range and on only one person at a time.

To deal with crowds of people, a German defense company is testing a "stun cannon." The new weapon uses an explosive charge to squirt a stream of tiny fibers through the air. The fibers then conduct a powerful stream of electricity. An American company has built a device called the Close Quarters Shock Rifle that works in a similar way. The shock rifle projects a long thread of glowing plasma to conduct a lightninglike electric beam.

When struck by the electric beam from one of these weapons, a person cannot move for several seconds but is otherwise not seriously hurt. The weapons can even stop a car or truck by disabling its electronic ignition system.

ACTIVE DENIAL

Another weapon that can disable a person without causing serious injury has an effect that is like dozens of hot light bulbs pressed against the skin. This device, called an active denial weapon, looks like a giant satellite dish. It fires a wide-angle beam of electromagnetic energy that heats water molecules in a person's

STICKY FOAM

To subdue a suspect, police might soon use a weapon that sprays a dark brown sludgy foam that clings to clothes, windows, and walls. The protein foam is made from a whipped concoction of ground-up hooves, horns, cartilage, and other beef by-products. Officers must be careful not to suffocate a suspect with the foam, but the disgusting stuff is actually safe enough to be ingested. Not surprisingly, however, it tastes terrible. The foam can be removed with a cloth or a spray of water. Left to dry, it flakes apart like huge pieces of dandruff.

The sticky-foam weapon resembles a flamethrower.

U.S. troops used a similar kind of foam to stop rioting crowds in Mogadishu, Somalia. Sprayed from backpack weapons that looked like flamethrowers, the sticky stuff was formed into thick barriers to hold back the rioters without harming them. While the tactic worked well at first, Somalis quickly learned they could build crude wooden ramps to clamber over the foam barriers. Some critics used the episode to argue that nonlethal weapons do not work and actually could endanger troops in the field by encouraging them to use insufficient force.

Supporters of the technology insist that the foam does have its uses, particularly in law enforcement. It could be sprayed to form a thick cocoon around the arms and legs of a violent suspect or applied in thick layers to the windows and doors of a trapped felon's house. Time will tell if sticky foam becomes a standard weapon in the arsenal of police and the military.

An active denial weapon can be mounted on a Humvee (pictured).

skin. The resulting pain is brief but very intense, rendering a victim helpless.

Inventors of the weapon, which can be mounted on a Humvee or large truck, claim it would be safe to use in subduing crowds and would not cause serious injuries. They claim that because active denial weapons heat the skin only to a depth of 0.64 inches (0.25cm), of an inch, they do not cause harmful burns. Critics, however, point out that the level of energy used could be increased very easily. Then, instead of a momentary sensation of heat, the victim would suffer a scalding burn that would cause permanent damage.

SONIC CANNONS

Besides disabling heat and electricity, inventors have also sought ways to harness sound as a weapon. The roar of a rock concert can have a percussive effect, like a punch in the stomach, and continuous loud noise can prevent a person from concentrating. These ideas are the basis for a nonlethal weapon called the sonic cannon.

From a box that looks like a stereo speaker, the device aims a stream of so-called sonic bullets along a narrow beam. The operator can choose from among several annoying sounds in the cannon's computer. One of the most effective is the high-pitched wailing of a

The sonic cannon uses the cries of a baby played backwards as one of its sonic-bullet sounds.

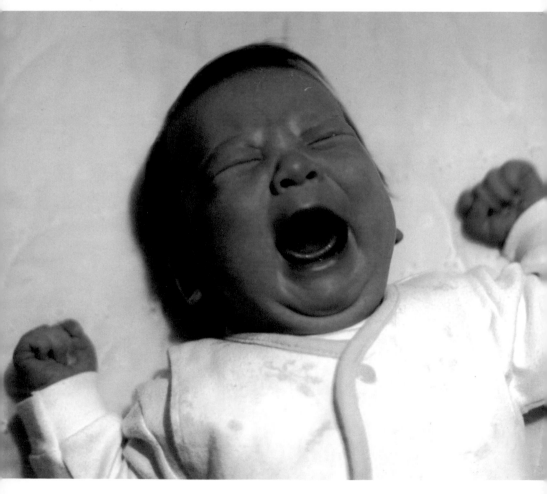

baby, played backwards. A person who enters the beam's path is assaulted with deafening noise. At 110 decibels, the ears start ringing and the skull begins to vibrate. When the beam is shut off, the sound instantly goes away.

The ability to aim the sonic bullets protects the weapon's operator from its effects. The sonic cannon would be especially effective in flushing adversaries out of an enclosed area such as a cave. Its beam ricochets the sound off of walls, thus multiplying an ear-piercing wail several times over. Victims would suffer no permanent damage from the weapon, although their ears might ring for several hours.

STINK BOMBS

Another area of research for nonlethal weapons is based on aromatherapy—but in reverse. Instead of finding scents that appeal to people, scientists are seeking the foulest odors on Earth. For researchers at the Monell Chemical Senses Center in Philadelphia, Pennsylvania, the worse something smells, the more useful it is to their work. The idea is a simple one: People tend to avoid places that smell bad.

So-called stink bombs are even less dangerous than tear gas and pepper spray, and are effective in very small doses. Finding the odors that work best, however, is a rather distasteful business. Scientists at the Monell Center have discovered that certain odors are repulsive to people of every culture. These tend to be smells with a biological connection: human waste, vomit, body odor, burning hair, and rotting garbage. Chemists create artificial mixtures of the vilest aromas and test them on human subjects.

For example, a scientist at Monell wanted to isolate the stench of decaying flesh. She took a dead mouse caught in a trap and wrapped it in a plastic bag to trap the scent. Then she used a syringe to collect particles from the rancid air in the bag. By

A scientist used the smell of a dead mouse caught in a trap to create an effective stink chemical.

analyzing the particles, chemists were able to isolate the chemical makeup of "rotting mouse." Finally, they mixed the precise chemicals to create their own essence of decaying mouse.

Test subjects were fitted with hoods inside which the mouse aroma, among others, was introduced. At the first sniff, their heads jerked back and their features twisted with disgust. Prolonged exposure made their heart rates soar and created strong feelings of nausea.

Researchers have not yet figured out precisely how to use this new technology. Perhaps someday important facilities will be guarded, and crowds will be dispersed, by these smelly, but nonlethal, weapons.

Whatever the future of stink bombs and other nonlethal weapons, it is clear that advances in weaponry will continue to be made. It remains to be seen, however, whether a trend toward less destructive weapons will grow, or if scientists will produce even more deadly weapons in the future.

GLOSSARY

active denial weapon A weapon that fires a beam of electromagnetic energy that heats the water molecules in a person's skin.

ASAT An antisatellite weapon designed to interfere with or eliminate a satellite or satellite communications.

blackout bomb A weapon that releases a mass of superconductive carbon filaments to disable power grids.

drone A pilotless aircraft.

E-bomb A weapon that produces a powerful burst of microwaves to disable electronic devices over a wide area; also called a microwave bomb.

electric-shock weapon A nonlethal weapon that can sweep a wide area with a powerful beam of electricity to incapacitate crowds of people.

Global Positioning System (GPS) A system that uses radio signals transmitted from satellites to fix the exact position of objects on Earth.

Joint Direct Attack Munition (JDAM) A guidance kit added to the tail of an old-style bomb to allow it to be guided by GPS data.

Micro Air Vehicle (MAV) A tiny, remote-controlled aircraft equipped with a camera and sensors.

napalm A jellied mixture of aluminum soap powder and gasoline used as an incendiary.

Packbot A small, remote-controlled robot used to search for mines and hidden explosives.

Patriot missile system A missile system designed to shoot down incoming strategic missiles using a combination of radar data and computer guidance.

smart weapons Weapons guided by laser, computer, and/or satellite data so as to be more accurate than conventional weapons.

sonic cannon A weapon that emits a beam of ultrasonic waves.

stink bomb A nonlethal weapon that emits a distasteful smell.

Tactical High Energy Laser (THEL) A weapon that produces a high-energy laser that can disable missiles at long range.

target designator A method of "painting" a target with a pulse of laser energy to lead a weapon to its goal.

FOR FURTHER INFORMATION

Books

Matthew Pitt, *The Tomahawk Cruise Missile*. New York: Childrens Press, 2000.

Jay Speakman, *Weapons of War*. San Diego: Lucent Books, 2001.

Web Sites

How Patriot Missiles Work (http://science.howstuffworks.com/patriot-missile.htm) A detailed description of the Patriot missile system.

Weapons of the United States Military (http://usmilitary.about.com/od/weapons). A collection of articles about U.S. military hardware, including many high-tech weapons.

INDEX

MiG, 15
Missiles, 4, 14, 18, 29
 see also Guided missiles
Mutually assured destruction (MAD), 14

Napalm, 17
Nonlethal weapons, 5, 35–43
Nuclear weapons, 6, 13, 14, 15, 29

Packbot, 27, 30
Panzer IV tank, 7–8
Patriot missile, 20–21
Pepper spray, 36, 41
Persian Gulf War, 20, 22, 23–24
P-40 Warhawk (fighter plane), 9
Planes, 7, 9–10, 15, 25
Predator, 25

Radar, 9, 21, 25
Radios, 8
Radio wave, 9, 19
Reconnaissance, 25
Robots, 27, 31–32
Rocket launchers, 15–16
Rockets, 11–12, 21

Sabre fighter jet, 15
Satellites, 5, 18, 19, 22, 25, 27, 29
Scud missiles, 20
Shock rifle, 37
Smart weapons, 22–24
Sonic cannons, 39–41
Space technology, 28–29
Spoofing, 29

Spy planes, 25
Star Wars, 18
Stink bombs, 41–43
Strategic Defense Initiative (SDI), 18,
 19, 20
Stun guns, 37
Super Bazooka, 16

Tanks, 6, 7–8, 15
Taser, 37
Tear gas, 35–36, 41
THEL (Tactical High Energy Laser),
 33
Thermo-corrosive bomb, 30–31
Tomahawk cruise missiles, 24
Two-way radios, 8
Type O Carrier Fighter, 9–10

Ultra (code), 9

Vietnam War, 15–17, 23
V-1 Flying Bomb, 11
V-2 Rocket, 12

Water cannons, 36
Weapons
 nonlethal, 35–43
 of today, 14–24
 of tomorrow, 25–34, 35–43
Weapons guidance systems, 28
World War I, 6, 17
World War II, 6–7, 7–13, 15

Zero (fighter plane), 9–10

ABOUT THE AUTHOR

John Allen is a writer who lives in Oklahoma City. He is the author of *Idi Amin* and *Robert Boyle,* also published by Blackbirch Press.